DIMENSIONS OF HEALTH

SOCIAL HEALTH

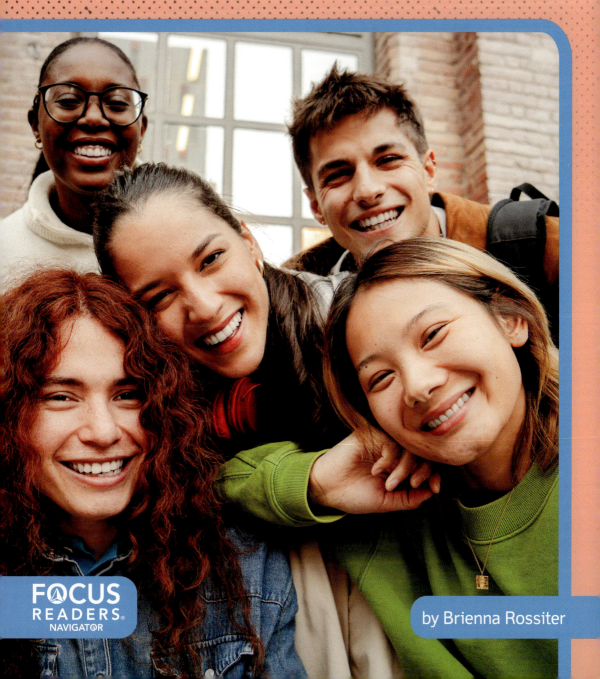

by Brienna Rossiter

WWW.FOCUSREADERS.COM

Copyright © 2026 by Focus Readers®, Mendota Heights, MN 55120. All rights reserved. No part of this book may be reproduced or utilized in any form or by any means without written permission from the publisher.

Focus Readers is distributed by North Star Editions:
sales@northstareditions.com | 888-417-0195

Produced for Focus Readers by Red Line Editorial.

Photographs ©: Shutterstock Images, cover, 1, 6, 8–9, 10, 12, 15, 16–17, 19, 20–21, 23, 25, 26–27; Travis Morisse/The Hutchinson News/AP Images, 4–5; iStockphoto, 28

Library of Congress Cataloging-in-Publication Data
Names: Rossiter, Brienna, author.
Title: Social health / by Brienna Rossiter.
Description: Mendota Heights, MN: Focus Readers, [2026] | Series: Dimensions of health | Includes index. | Audience: Grades 4-6
Identifiers: LCCN 2024059374 (print) | LCCN 2024059375 (ebook) | ISBN 9798889985280 (hardcover) | ISBN 9798889985884 (pdf) | ISBN 9798889985600 (ebook)
Subjects: LCSH: Social interaction--Psychological aspects--Juvenile literature. | Social interaction--Health aspects--Juvenile literature. | Interpersonal relations--Psychological aspects--Juvenile literature. | Well-being--Juvenile literature.
Classification: LCC HM1111 .R677 2026 (print) | LCC HM1111 (ebook) | DDC 302--dc23/eng/20250123
LC record available at https://lccn.loc.gov/2024059374
LC ebook record available at https://lccn.loc.gov/2024059375

Printed in the United States of America
Mankato, MN
082025

ABOUT THE AUTHOR
Brienna Rossiter is a writer and editor who lives in Minnesota.

TABLE OF CONTENTS

CHAPTER 1
Connecting at Camp 5

CHAPTER 2
What Is Social Health? 9

CONNECTIONS
Friendship and Feelings 14

CHAPTER 3
Healthy or Unhealthy? 17

CHAPTER 4
What to Look For 21

CHAPTER 5
Action Steps 27

Focus Questions • 30
Glossary • 31
To Learn More • 32
Index • 32

CHAPTER 1

CONNECTING AT CAMP

A girl signs up for an art camp at a nature center near her home. On the first day, she feels a bit nervous. When her mom drops her off, several kids are already in the classroom. They stand in a circle, talking.

The girl takes a deep breath. She walks over and introduces herself. She learns

> Many nature centers offer camps and classes. They teach people about science and the natural world.

 Exploring a trail or lake at a local park can be a fun way to be active with others.

each person's name. Then she asks what they like to do. She learns that they all enjoy swimming. The girl tells them that she does, too.

Later that morning, the kids go for a hike. They find leaves and use them to make prints. The next day, they draw wildflowers. Each day, the girl gets to know her classmates better. She asks questions and listens closely as people answer. By the end of the week, she has made several new friends.

ACTIVE WITH OTHERS

Exercise is good for people's health. So is spending time with others. Blending the two can be especially helpful. People can join groups that play sports. They can take classes to learn karate or yoga. They can walk or bike with friends. Being outdoors often has the most benefits. People can look for nearby trails or parks.

CHAPTER 2

WHAT IS SOCIAL HEALTH?

Social health is about a person's relationships. It measures how connected a person feels to others. Some relationships are between two people. However, many involve groups. Some groups, such as families, are relatively small. But people are also part of larger communities. Examples include schools,

Having fun with others helps increase people's sense of belonging.

 People with strong connections are less likely to have certain health problems. These include depression, dementia, and heart disease.

neighborhoods, workplaces, and places of worship.

A person's social health is shaped by how many groups they are part of. It also involves how the person feels about their relationships. People with good social health tend to have many strong ties to others. They feel supported and cared for.

Good social health has many benefits. People with strong connections tend to live longer. Their **mental health** tends to be better. They are better able to deal with pain and loss. And they tend to have lower levels of **stress**.

In contrast, loneliness and isolation are both linked to poor health. Isolated

LONELINESS SURVEY

Age	Percentage
AGE 15-18	25%
AGE 19-29	27%
AGE 30-44	25%
AGE 45-64	22%
AGE 65+	17%

Between June 2022 and February 2023, a survey asked people in more than 140 countries if they felt lonely. This graph shows how many said yes.

People who have been hurt or afraid in social situations may try to avoid being around other people.

people are often alone. They have few relationships. Loneliness is more about how someone feels. Lonely people may be around others. But they don't feel close to them. People who are lonely or isolated tend not to live as long. And they are at greater risk for some types of disease.

Certain types of people are more likely to be lonely or isolated. For some people, making friends doesn't come easily. They feel anxious in groups. It's harder for them to feel like they fit in. People from **marginalized** groups are also at higher risk of being lonely or isolated. When people have less **access** to **resources**, connecting with others is harder.

ACCESS MATTERS

Where a person lives can play a big role in their social health. For example, people in rural areas often live far from others. And in cities, some people don't have cars. If they don't live near a bus route, getting around can be difficult. They are more likely to be isolated. Safe public areas, such as parks and libraries, provide places for people to gather. People who live near them are less likely to feel lonely.

> CONNECTIONS

FRIENDSHIP AND FEELINGS

Social health and emotional health are closely connected. Emotional health is being able to understand and manage one's emotions. Emotionally healthy people can name what they are feeling. They also know helpful ways to process it.

For example, suppose someone is feeling stressed. An unhealthy response would be snapping at others. But emotional health would mean noticing the feeling. Then, the person could take steps to calm it. They might take deep breaths or go for a walk.

Emotional health is a key part of building and maintaining relationships. People who understand emotions make good friends. They think about how their words and actions affect others. They

Being emotionally healthy helps people support friends who are going through hard times.

may still feel sad or angry. But they try not to take it out on other people.

Emotional health also helps people notice what others are feeling. They can then help others process those feelings. Knowing that others will be there to help when you need it is called emotional support. It's a key part of what makes people feel connected.

CHAPTER 3

HEALTHY OR UNHEALTHY?

People with more connections to others tend to have better social health. But the type of relationship also matters. Not all relationships are healthy. And unhealthy relationships have many negative impacts. They increase stress. They can harm mental health. They can even make people more likely to get sick.

> Unhealthy relationships can happen in person or online.

Knowing what healthy relationships look like is important. In a healthy relationship, both people feel seen and cared about. They take turns listening and helping. And they treat each other with respect. Conflict can still happen. But people admit when they are wrong and say they are sorry. It's not healthy for one person to never listen or apologize.

In healthy relationships, people can share their honest thoughts. And they can set boundaries. In some unhealthy relationships, one person tries to control the other. This person is often angry or demanding. The other person may feel like they can't disagree or say no.

A therapist can help people process painful experiences and learn to build healthy relationships.

Think about the relationships in your life. If any are unhealthy, you may need to step back. If you're not sure how to do that, ask for help. Talk to a friend or trusted adult. Parents or teachers may be able to give advice. Or they can help find an expert, such as a therapist, who knows more.

CHAPTER 4

WHAT TO LOOK FOR

Y ou can ask yourself questions to **evaluate** your social health. For example, how much time do you spend with others? Do those groups or relationships make you feel loved and supported? Are all your relationships very similar? Or do you know people from a variety of places and backgrounds?

> Friends, family, neighbors, and classmates all play a role in a person's social health.

Each person is different. The answers will vary. So will the answers that promote health. Some people enjoy getting to know lots of people. They like being part of many activities and doing things in big groups. Other people prefer having a few close friends.

FACE TO FACE

Many people connect with others online or by texting. Both can be good tools. They offer ways to meet people with shared interests. And they help people who live far apart stay in touch. But having in-person interactions is also important. Studies have found that people receive more support from people that they see in real life. And when two people meet face to face, their brains release chemicals that lower stress and pain.

Phones can help people have fun with friends. But checking phones too much makes it harder to pay attention to others.

There's not just one way to be healthy. It's about knowing yourself and what works for you.

However, a few things help make all relationships strong. One is listening carefully. When someone is talking, it's easy to start thinking about what you want to say next. But that can make the person feel unimportant. Instead, give your full attention. This shows you care.

Communicating clearly is also important. Part of good social health is being honest. Practice saying what you think and feel. It's okay to disagree or say no. But stay respectful. Show kindness with your words and tone of voice.

Meeting new people is a great way to build connections. For some people, doing this can be scary. It can help to shift the focus to others. If you feel nervous, look for another person to talk to. Try to make that person feel

In a healthy friendship, both people take turns listening to and helping each other.

comfortable. Ask them questions. You will often end up feeling connected.

However, one person shouldn't do all the work. Make sure you have the support you need. It's also okay to take time by yourself.

CHAPTER 5

ACTION STEPS

There are many ways to make new connections. One is joining a group or class. You can try something new. Or you can meet others who share a hobby.

Volunteering helps, too. You can help at a local park, library, or **nonprofit**. There, you can meet others with similar values. And you can give back to the community.

> People who like music can meet others by joining a band or choir.

Keeping parks clean and accessible helps people be active and make new friends.

In fact, you can help the whole community be healthier. For example, when public parks are safe and easy to use, people spend more time outdoors together. **Public transportation** also helps people connect. So, you can support laws that improve parks and transportation. You can call or write lawmakers. When more people have access, the whole community benefits.

You can also strengthen your existing connections. You can reach out and show you care. You can send messages or letters. Or your family can plan a get-together with neighbors. Bringing people together helps everyone improve their social health.

SPREADING KINDNESS

A bully is someone who hurts or **belittles** others. This can happen in person or online. People who are bullied are much more likely to be lonely or isolated. If you see bullying happen, don't join in. Tell an adult. And encourage your friends not to make fun of others. That way, more people will feel like they belong.

FOCUS QUESTIONS

Write your answers on a separate piece of paper.

1. Write a paragraph describing what a healthy relationship looks like.

2. Do you prefer hanging out in a big group or with just a few friends? Why?

3. Which phrase describes a person who is isolated?
    - A. someone with many relationships
    - B. someone with few relationships
    - C. someone who sees many people but doesn't feel close to them

4. What effect would closing a city park have on people's social health?
    - A. People would be less likely to become isolated.
    - B. People would be more likely to become isolated.
    - C. People would become more socially healthy.

Answer key on page 32.

GLOSSARY

access
The opportunity to use something or benefit from it.

belittles
Makes someone feel disliked and unimportant.

evaluate
To think carefully about how good or bad something is.

marginalized
Part of a group that does not have much power and is often ignored or treated as less important.

mental health
How well or unwell someone's mind is, including their emotions and thinking.

nonprofit
An organization that does work it believes is important instead of focusing on making money.

public transportation
Systems used for travel, such as buses and subways.

resources
Things, such as money or transportation, that help people meet needs or solve problems.

stress
A feeling of tension or pressure caused by the things going on around someone.

TO LEARN MORE

BOOKS

Gagne, Tammy. *Developing Relationship Skills*. BrightPoint Press, 2023.

Knutson, Julie. *Do the Work! Good Health and Well-Being*. Cherry Lake Publishing, 2022.

Kukla, Lauren. *Connect with Art! Activities to Strengthen Relationships*. Abdo Publishing, 2023.

NOTE TO EDUCATORS

Visit **www.focusreaders.com** to find lesson plans, activities, links, and other resources related to this title.

INDEX

bullying, 29

classes, 7, 27
communities, 9, 27–29

emotional health, 14–15
exercise, 7

families, 9, 29
friends, 7, 12, 14, 19, 22, 29

healthy relationships, 18

isolation, 11–13, 29

listening, 7, 18, 23
loneliness, 11–13, 29

mental health, 11

parks, 7, 13, 27–28
public transportation, 28

resources, 13

stress, 11, 14, 17, 22

therapist, 19

unhealthy relationships, 17–19

volunteering, 27